MEDIA FOCUS

Sandy Levin
WEST ELGIN SECONDARY SCHOOL
RICHMOND HILL, ONTARIO

Copp Clark Pitman Ltd.
A Longman Company
Toronto

ISBN 0-7730-4975-4

Every reasonable attempt has been made to trace the owners of copyright material used in this book. Any errors or omissions brought to the publisher's attention will be rectified in future printings.

The editors would like to acknowledge the advice of John Travers Coleman, President of the Canadian Advertising Foundation.

CANADIAN CATALOGUING IN PUBLICATION DATA

Levin, Sandy, 1955–
  Advertising

(Media focus)
ISBN 0-7730-4975-4

1. Advertising. 2. Advertising — Problems, exercises, etc. I. Title. II. Series.

HF5823.L48 1991   659.1   C90-095435-3

Editing: *Sheila Fletcher*
Photo Research: *Melanie Sherwood*
Cover and Text Design: *Holly Fisher & Associates*
Cover Illustration: *Kim LaFave*
Typesetting: *Compeer Typographic Services Ltd.*
Printing and Binding: *T.H. Best Printing Company*

Copp Clark Pitman Ltd.
2775 Matheson Blvd. East
Mississauga, Ont.
L4W 4P7

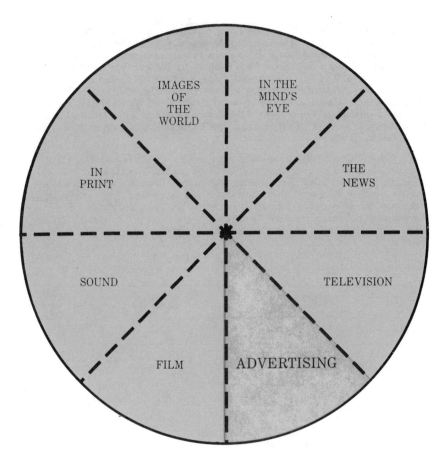

The mass media are the various means we use to communicate ideas and information to large audiences throughout the world. Today, almost any event occurring anywhere in the world can become common knowledge at the touch of a button or the turn of a page. Thus, the mass media have helped turn our world into a "global village."

With so much information from various media bombarding us, we need a means to analyse and organize it so that we can deal with it.

Media Focus will help you acquire an understanding of the various media and how they affect you every day.

The publisher would like to thank the following companies and agencies for permission to reprint their advertisements: Mediacom, Compaq/Computer Corp., CNCP, Ontario Ministry of Health and Welfare, Procter and Gamble, Canadian Children's Foundation, Daily Bread Food Bank, Metro Works Department, TransAd, Animation House, Ikea, Star Kist Foods Canada, Kimberley-Clark Canada, Canadian Cancer Society, Paramount Holidays, Kiku Restaurant, Insignia Group, Air Canada, Foodland Ontario, Canadian Airlines, Nissan Canada, World Wildlife Fund, Nike Canada, Newfoundland Department of Development and Tourism, Club Med Canada, Popsicle Industries, CIBC, The Globe and Mail, Eastman Kodak Company, Canapress Photo Service (p. 93).

Hugh Winsor, "Government advertising to sell budget . . ." *Globe and Mail*, 8 May 1989, A2. Reprinted with permission of The Globe and Mail. Greg Quill, "The world according to commercials," *Toronto Star*, 30 July 1988. Reprinted with permission — The Toronto Star Syndicate. "What advertising and image can do" or "The selling of fragrance" from *Co-ed* (Nov./Dec. 1984). © 1984 by Scholastic Inc. Reprinted by permission of Scholastic, Inc. Dave Chenoweth, "How to make a TV commercial," Montreal *Gazette*, 20 September 1980. Reprinted by permission of the Montreal Gazette.

CONTENTS

ADVERTISING

WHAT IS ADVERTISING?

A STATE OF MIND Levi's

Have you ever noticed ads for this product (or products like this)? How do you react to the ads? Are they appealing or not? Do they make the product attractive to you? In what way? Is there anything about any of these ads that you dislike? If you could afford them, would you choose to buy these products? Why or why not?

The answers that people like you give to questions such as these are important to the people involved in North America's multi-billion dollar advertising industry.

Advertising is the paid use of a **medium** (such as television, radio, magazines, billboards, or newspapers) to communicate a message to a **target market** (the audience the advertiser wants the ad to reach).

Advertising is perhaps the most familiar way media are used to communicate. No wonder. By the time you reach adulthood, you will have seen and heard nearly half a million advertising messages promoting the use of a particular airline, the consumption of a particular brand of soft drink, the wise use of energy, or the benefits of voting for a particular political party. Because it has the power to influence so many aspects of our lives, advertising attracts a great deal of attention from governments trying to regulate its use, from businesses trying to use it more effectively, and from consumers trying to make their way through all its conflicting claims. For this reason, it is important that you, as a consumer, take a close look at the world of advertising.

Why Advertise?

Everyone knows that the answer to the question, Why advertise? is to get people to buy a product or service. Within that generalization, however, are some more specific responses to the question. For example, suppose you and others in your apartment building or on your block are planning a lawn sale. In order to get people to buy, you would probably produce advertising flyers in which you might do some or all of the following:

- communicate a sales message
- provide information
- give location
- remind customers
- persuade consumers

LAWN SALE!

NEW AND USED HOUSEHOLD ITEMS

154 PATHWAY DRIVE

SATURDAY, 13 MAY

10:00 A.M. – 4:00 P.M.

This is the annual lawn sale event. Remember last year's bargains.

Don't Miss Out!
Low, Low Prices!
Bargains Galore!

Different companies and organizations have different reasons for advertising. An organization may advertise to increase sales or participation in an activity, improve its image, inform the public, or to introduce itself, a new product, or a new service.

1. Increase Sales or Participation

Most of the advertising you see is created for profit-making businesses. It is created and exhibited to promote the purchase of goods, the use of services, and the acceptance of ideas. The message communicated in the advertising may remind consumers to buy or use products or services they already utilize. Advertisers feel this reinforcement is necessary for continued success.

Advertising also reminds recent purchasers that they made a good buying decision. It has been shown, for example, that car buyers continue to look at advertising for the vehicle after the purchase, simply to reassure themselves they made the right choice.

Advertisers also encourage consumers to increase their use of a product or service. For example, the makers of Peek Freans cookies discovered that many people bought the cookies for special occasions only. The company and its advertising agency, Saatchi & Saatchi, Compton, Hayhurst, developed a series of ads that showed people eating the cookies on special occasions that were not really so special (a goldfish's birthday, for example).

Unlike profit-making businesses, non-profit organizations advertise to increase the participation in an event, or the amount of giving.

Advertising also encourages consumers to switch brands. Companies that offer similar products or services (e.g., computers, airlines, automobiles) often try to encourage customers to switch from a competitor's product or service. The goal of such advertising is to persuade consumers that the product or service of one company is better or different by showing the benefits of switching.

Often you will see advertising that directly compares one product or service to its competitors. This is called **comparative advertising**. It is legal and often used by companies that have a strong, easily identified competitor to challenge.

2. Improve the Image

A second reason why an organization might advertise is to improve its image. This kind of advertising is called **institutional or corporate advertising**. Such advertising usually stresses the efficiency, friendliness, security, or good corporate citizenship of the company. It may be aimed at customers, employees, share-

Ad Note

holders, governments, and other groups affected by the actions of the company.

3. Inform the Public

Organizations may also advertise in order to inform the public. For example, the largest advertisers in Canada are governments. They advertise in various media to inform and communicate with the public about a wide variety of issues. The federal government may wish to inform the public about changes in an existing program. During tax time, governments advertise to tell people what they need to know in order to complete a tax return.

Some people feel that governments should not spend taxpayers' money for some kinds of advertising. Read the following column by Hugh Winsor of *The Globe and Mail*. What does he feel should be the purpose of government advertising?

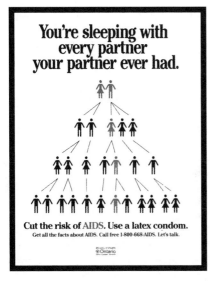

Government advertising also delivers powerful messages on health and welfare.

Government advertising to sell budget shows only one side of coin

BY HUGH WINSOR THE GLOBE AND MAIL

Ottawa hockey fans could be forgiven for thinking the large coin that rolled across their television screens with the chunk out of it was some new promotion for Sudbury's Big Nickel — if it weren't for the little red maple leaf and the Government of Canada sign at the bottom.

No, what is happening, according to Finance Minister Michael Wilson, is that viewers are being "educated," with $2.7 million of their own money, about the evils of deficits and debt and why they should accept, in the spirit of the Victory Bonds of the war years, the tough new taxes he dished up for them last week.

"I think it is very important Canadians understand the nature of the problem we are facing," he told reporters in defending the propaganda campaign.

The ads — like the geese and beavers that were supposed to give us a warm feeling in the tummy about the Constitution in the early eighties, and the "Just that close" pinched-finger ads run about oil self-sufficiency by former Liberal energy minister Marc Lalonde — are attempts at social engineering. They are supposed to build a constituency for a particular policy or philosophy of the government of the day by using one of the most potent of modern communication techniques, television advertising, paid for, of course, by the people being engineered.

Both the morality and the efficacy of such interventionist thrusts have been called into question.

It is a practice "which we believe constitutes a grave abuse of both Parliament and of public funds," thundered one prominent parliamentarian. "In many cases, the advertising used is designed not to inform the public of Canada, but to misinform the public of Canada."

An equally senior politician had this to say about the government's use of advocacy advertising to promote its policies: "If you were running a corporation in the private sector, for example, General Motors or General Foods, you would have a responsibility to sell your product, to get out and hustle in the market place, to develop a good corporate image to convince Canadians that your product was better than the competition . . . By contrast, the prime responsibility of the federal government should not be to sell a product but rather to inform Canadians about the law, about changes in the law, about their rights, about health programs and about how programs work so that services can be provided. . . . We should scrap federal advocacy advertising. The time has come to draw the line and to say that this must stop.''

Tough stuff — and it applies appropriately to the debt-coin ads, because this advertising blitz refers to no law that has been passed by Parliament. Nor does it make any reference to the rights or programs to which taxpayers might be entitled.

What a pity that neither of the two speakers — External Affairs Minister Joe Clark in the first instance and Health Minister Perrin Beatty in the second, who made these points when former prime minister Pierre Trudeau was soft-soaping us about the Constitution — repeated their views when Mr. Wilson's new debt campaign was discussed at the cabinet table. How soon they forget the wisdom they had in opposition!

Because Mr. Wilson, who is usually more modest and conventional in the way he chooses to deliver his message, seems to have ignored his colleagues' former views about the morality of such advocacy, let us take a look at its effectiveness. There is an old adage in economics called Gresham's law that says bad coin drives out the good.

If the viewers decide that this blatant attempt at engineering their opinions is an insult to their intelligence, it could quickly become the bad coin that drives out any gains Mr. Wilson may have made in his debt sermons.

Instead of the coin with the big bite out of it to represent the tax dollars that go to finance Canada's accumulated debt, how about footage of passengers clogging the departure gates at Pearson airport with the message that taxpayers should fly, with the federal subsidy being only $35 a passenger trip, instead of taking Via Rail, where the subsidy is $90 a trip?

If we are serious about ''educating'' the taxpayer about where the dollars go, how about some footage of subsidized locomotives rolling out of the Bombardier shops, or planes rolling off the Boeing Downsview assembly line? Why not a shot of the General Motors factory in St. Therese, Que., or the new Domtar pulp mill at Windsor, Que.? The price tags all start at $100 million, at least.

If we had the U.S. provision that allows the right to respond to advocacy advertising, the answering ads could show a team of decorators and furniture salesmen in the various cabinet ministers' offices.

Or, on a more serious note, a shot of Clarence Barber, professor emeritus at the University of Manitoba, who had taken on all of the doomsayers who hold that nothing positive comes out of government debt. He estimates the growth of government debt has added at least $150 billion of safe marketable securities to the portfolios of business firms and individuals in Canada. Not only does it provide an opportunity and income for savers, but it has also strengthened the financial position of the private sector and has contributed to the recovery of Canadian capital spending.

This might just show that the debt Mr. Wilson is concerned about is a two-sided coin. ■

4. Introduce a Company, Product, Service

A fourth reason for advertising is so that a new company can gain recognition as well as present its new product or new service.

Look at the following ads.

When the Canadian Children's Foundation started the Kids Help Phone, ads ran on television, radio, as well as in transit shelters.

Advertising: What's Good About It?

Advertising has the ability to make you laugh, to make you cry, to irritate you, and, sometimes, to make you downright mad! Some of you may love advertising, and some may hate it. Whatever your opinion, advertising does have some distinct advantages as far as you, the consumer, are concerned. For example, companies pay newspapers, magazines, and television and radio stations to carry their advertising. How much would you be prepared to pay for your favourite magazine? Would you be prepared to pay for a TV licence each year? Thanks to advertising, the consumer does not have to pay the entire cost of magazine production or TV service.

Advertising through mass media is the quickest way to introduce something to the public. Without advertising to communicate with potential customers, companies would likely use more expensive methods such as personal selling. It is likely that this higher cost would be passed on to the consumer in higher prices.

How often have you seen a new product advertised and thought to yourself, "Hm, that looks good — I'll have to try it"? You are only one among millions who may be reacting the same way to that ad. Because advertising can quickly reach a mass audience, it can help create a demand for new goods and services. Developing and introducing new goods and services is very expensive, and many new products fail. Without advertising, even more would fail. Thus, advertising helps provide us with new goods and services which, in their turn, provide jobs for more people.

In addition, advertising itself provides many jobs. People at advertising agencies, at newspapers, magazines, television and radio stations work with advertising every day.

Advertising: The Down Side

Advertising does have its critics. Some critics argue that advertising forces people to buy things they do not want. What do you think? Have you ever bought items you saw advertised and then felt "conned" because you purchased something you didn't really want?

Some advertisers insist that a great deal of advertising is nothing more than an effort to get consumers to switch from the brand they are currently using to the brand being advertised. Critics point out that this claim means that advertising is money wasted, because the actual amount of the product or service being used does not increase. A study found that advertising for such products as beer, autos, soap, and pain relievers, does not seem to have much effect on total sales of these products.

Other critics argue that advertising is limited to promoting the sales of goods and services, rather than for the betterment of society as a whole.

Critics of advertising also point to examples in which millions of dollars of advertising have not helped a company's sales. The mid-1980s saw two fiascos: the introduction of the "New" Coke, and the $40 million "Where's Herb?" advertising campaign from Burger King. Neither ad campaign had much success increasing demand for the product.

Whatever your opinion about it, advertising will continue to generate discussion for many years to come. What is important is for you to become more aware of advertising, and of the techniques used by advertisers. You have seen something of the "what" and "why" of advertising. In the next section, you will learn more about the media used by advertisers.

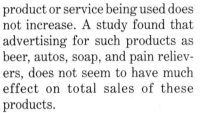

AD BREAK

Ad Info:
1. What is advertising?
2. Why is it important that you take a closer look at the world of advertising?
3. What are the four major reasons why an organization might advertise?
4. What is one advantage to consumers of advertising? What is one disadvantage?

Ad Data:
1. Reread the article by Hugh Winsor.

    a) What is the advertising that he objects to called?

    b) Americans who disagree with such advertising can do something that Canadians cannot. What is it?

    c) What is Mr. Winsor's opinion of this form of advertising? Explain why you agree or disagree with Mr. Winsor's opinion.

2. William Wrigley, Jr., chewing gum manufacturer, was travelling on a train with a company accountant. The accountant suggested to Mr. Wrigley that he reduce the amount of money spent on advertising. Mr. Wrigley replied first by asking the accountant "How fast is this train going?" The accountant answered, "About 100 kilometres per hour." Wrigley then asked, "Then why doesn't the railroad remove the engine and let the train travel on its own?"

    a) What was Mr. Wrigley trying to tell the accountant about the importance of advertising?

    b) What would Wrigley try to accomplish through advertising?

    c) What do you think of William Wrigley, Jr.'s answer to the accountant's question? Was it a good answer? Why or why not?

3. What other advantages and disadvantages to advertising can you think of besides those you have read in the text?

4. Find three examples of comparative advertising on radio or television or in print. Do the ads convince you to switch? Why or why not? If not, what would you change in the advertising to convince consumers to switch?

5. Find five examples of advertising for a new product or service. Include in your search those products which are new and improved. Note the product or service and where you saw or heard the ad.

6. Some critics argue that advertising is limited to promoting the sale of goods and services, and does not attempt the betterment of society as a whole. Should advertising be geared toward the betterment of society as a whole? Discuss.

Ad Write:
You are a rising star in an advertising agency. Your client is an

established company which is about to introduce a new product. You have to deal with an accountant whose attitude is similar to that of William Wrigley, Jr.'s. Write a memo (or a letter) to persuade this accountant to put more money into advertising existing products, (she says they are well established, so they do not need advertising), or to spend money on a major ad campaign for the new product (she says the company name will be enough to gain acceptance for the new product). Can you think of any clever ways to be persuasive, as William Wrigley, Jr. did? ∎

THE ADVERTISING MEDIA

Selecting which medium to use depends to some extent on the consumers the advertiser wishes to reach. The medium or media selected must be seen or heard by the target market. If a company's target market is teenage males, it is unlikely that many of them will be reading *Chatelaine* or *Epicure*. If the target market is a city dweller, it's unlikely that ads appealing to that market would appear in the dairy farmer's *Holstein Journal*. The fact that such specialty magazines exist should indicate to you that there is a way to deliver an advertising message to almost any audience. In this section you will look at the media with which you, as consumers, are probably the most familiar:

- television
- radio
- newspapers
- magazines
- outdoor advertising
- transit advertising

If you were an advertiser, how would you decide which medium to use? You would have to ask yourself questions such as, "How much money do I need to spend for advertising?" "Is my product technical in nature?" "Should the consumer see it being used?" Once the advertising target has been determined and the message has been decided, it is time to select the medium. If the consumer needs to see the product or service being used, a visual medium is necessary. If the product being advertised is technical in nature, the print media may be best. A company's message must also be seen or heard enough times to make an impact. If the budget is limited, it may be better to avoid television. An advertiser may get more exposure for the money using some of the other media. In order to make an informed decision, it is necessary to know something about each medium.

Television

Television is part of nearly everyone's life. Almost all Canadian households have a television and over half have more than one. During an average day, 80 percent of Canadians watch one or more of the over 100 Canadian and American television stations at least once.

Television stations are either part of a network (CBC, CTV, or Global) or independent, such as TVOntario, Access Alberta, and M.I.T. in the Maritimes. Advertising on network television is arranged centrally so that a national advertiser runs an ad over the network in the same time slot, usually on the same day, everywhere in the country. (In the case of local networks such as Global Television or TV Air Quebec, an ad will run in a region of the country.) This takes a great deal of planning. Advertising schedules for the national television networks are booked more than one year in advance, on noncancellable contracts.

The broadcasting day is divided into time slots called dayparts. The daypart with the largest audi-

ence is called prime time. It is dominated by those shows with the highest ratings. Ratings are used by the television advertising industry to measure the success of a program. The most popular shows have the greatest number of people watching them. The larger the audience, the higher the ratings, and the more advertisers are willing to pay for a time slot.

Before deciding whether or not to use television advertising, an advertiser must understand its strengths and weaknesses.

Strengths and Weaknesses of Television Advertising

Strengths	Weaknesses
• quickly reaches mass audience	• each commercial competes with many others for the viewer's attention
• can reach specific target markets (e.g. children on Saturday morning)	• advertisers are allowed only a limited amount of time each hour
• can evoke emotional response by telling "story" complete with sights and sounds	• less exposure for commercials because people are watching less network TV (watching more rented movies on VCRs)
• effective because it interrupts what consumers are doing	• viewers are free to leave the room
	• technology allows people to fast-forward or mute commercials
	• TV commercials are costly to make
	• TV air time is costly compared to other media

Ad Note

Making television commercials can be very expensive. On average, the cost of producing a commercial prepared for national broadcasting will be over $100 000. Costs can go much higher. Molson's spent over a half million dollars to shoot a commercial in Australia. In the early 1980s, Pepsi paid singer Michael Jackson $5 million to appear in just two advertisements.

In addition to the cost of making a commercial, advertising time is expensive. Advertising during a popular prime time television show is particularly expensive. Even more expensive are time slots during special events such as the Olympics or football's Super Bowl. One minute of advertising time during this year's Super Bowl will cost a company well over $1 000 000!

Radio

Although television advertising is widely used and recognized, many companies and organizations use radio in their advertising plans. There are over 700 AM and FM radio stations in Canada. Many radio stations are owned by corporations that have stations in many cities. Like television, radio reaches almost all Canadian households. On average, every Canadian over the age of eighteen listens to radio for nearly 20 hours per week.

Radio stations choose the music they play based on both the target market they wish to reach and the type of licence they hold from the CRTC. For example, almost all major cities have a Top 40 station that plays the most popular hits. The target market is a wide audience of adults, aged 25–45.

As is true for television, the radio day is divided into dayparts. People tune in most frequently during the morning drive time, from 6:00 a.m. to 10:00 a.m., Monday to Friday. For this reason, commercials are more expensive

Ad Note

Regulations for commercials are different for AM and FM radio stations. AM stations are self-regulating, and have no restrictions on the number of commercial minutes. FM stations are allowed 150 commercial minutes per day with no restrictions on the number per hour or the number of commercial breaks.

23

during this time, as well as more frequent.

Like television, radio, too, has its strengths and weaknesses.

Strengths and Weaknesses of Radio Advertising

Strengths	Weaknesses
• reaches many people • wide variety of stations can target different listeners • can be produced and aired quickly • production is relatively inexpensive • air time is relatively inexpensive	• limited advertising time available • limited effectiveness due to lack of visuals and motion • radios often produce only "background noise," so advertising is ignored

Newspapers

Despite the wide reach of the electronic media, the amount of money spent on print advertising is quite large.

There are over 100 daily newspapers in Canada, with a combined daily **circulation** (number of papers sold) of over 5 million.

Roughly 90 percent of all Canadian households read at least one newspaper per week. On average, nearly 70 percent of all adults read one newspaper per day, and almost 80 percent read a weekend paper.

The free-standing insert is the third main type of newspaper advertising. These advertisements are printed for an advertiser and then inserted into a newspaper. Retail stores usually have weekly inserts. Other advertisers also use inserts.

THE TOP TEN	
	Average Daily Circulation
The Toronto Star	562 000
Le Journal de Montreal	334 000
Toronto Globe and Mail	326 000
Toronto Sun	299 000
Vancouver Sun	244 000
Montreal La Presse	221 000
Montreal Gazette	211 000
Ottawa Citizen	205 000
Vancouver Province	187 000
Winnipeg Free Press	176 000

There are three main types of newspaper advertising — **classified, display** and **free-standing** inserts.

Display advertising uses both words and illustrations. Display advertising appears in almost every part of the paper.

HOMES FOR RENT

ON THE WATERFRONT! Beaut. 3 bed. th. Lots of extras. $3000/mo. Call 555-1000.

Lux. home east end. 4 bed. park. air. $2775/ mo. 842-2222 days.

DOWNTOWN. Single fam. home. 5 appl. long-term. 444-6000.

Moncton. What a find!! 5 bed. Lux. Gorgeous inside. $430/wk. 624-2662

CARS FOR SALE

1990 VOLKS. CORRADO Ex. cond. 222-6446.

1989 Mazda 323 65 k. $8000. 824-2119.

1988 Mustang. Going cheap. 888-5500.

Newspaper advertising, too, has its strengths and weaknesses.

Strengths and Weaknesses of Newspaper Advertising

Strengths	Weaknesses
• flexibility–easy to change ad	• many ads compete with each other
• newspapers are passed around so more people see the advertising	• some readers don't read all sections
• local audience responds to local business ads	• much newspaper advertising is black and white and is therefore less eye-catching
• low cost	• difficulty of demonstrating a product or showing motion
• readers more highly educated, so probably more affluent	

Magazines

The other well-known print advertising medium is the magazine. There are roughly 1500 consumer and business magazines published in Canada. Each year, over four billion copies of magazines are circulated. Canadian consumers spend over $500 million annually buying magazines. Consumers with the most years of schooling buy the most magazines. As well, higher income consumers spend more for magazines than lower income consumers.

Each magazine has a specific editorial policy which controls the type of articles which appear. The editorial policy selected is based on the target market of the magazine. For example, *Canadian Business* has articles of interest to the business community. *Maclean's* has articles of interest to the general public.

Strengths and Weaknesses of Magazine Advertising

Strengths	Weaknesses
• advertisers reach specific markets through specialty magazines	• long lead time–ad must be received by magazine as much as two months in advance of publication
• split runs provide a way of putting different ads in the same magazine in different cities	• colour reproduction costs make much magazine advertising expensive
• magazine size can increase to accommodate more ads	• magazines are usually printed monthly, giving minimal exposure to an ad
• magazines may be reread and passed around, so that an ad may be seen repeatedly	• no sound and motion

Outdoor Advertising

Although you may well know billboards, outdoor advertising includes the following six types:

Billboards

Backlights

Superboards

Transit shelters

Mall posters

Airport posters

Strengths and Weaknesses of Poster Advertising

Strengths	Weaknesses
• seen many times (Avg. 33 times a month) • can't be turned off • advertiser can select location • can be unique and very creative	• lead time; artwork required five weeks in advance • must be brief • national advertising can be expensive • limited amount of space available

Transit Advertising

Do you ride a bus, a streetcar, or the subway to school? If you do, chances are you are very familiar with transit advertising. Transit advertising refers to the ads that appear in and on public transportation vehicles and stations.

Nearly all Canadian transit advertising is handled by one company, Trans Ad. Trans Ad offers space in and on transit vehicles and facilities. Trans Ad does not print or create the advertising, but manages their posting and placement. Revenue is shared between the transit system and Trans Ad.

Transit advertising is actually a variety of products which can be grouped into two basic categories: exterior and interior, with interior sub-divided into transit cards and subway products.

Ad Note

In Toronto, buses are based in locations called barns. Buses travel certain routes from each barn, and return there each night. If desired, an advertiser can buy space only on the buses that are housed in certain barns.

Strengths and Weaknesses of Transit Advertising

Strengths	Weaknesses
• reasonable rates • continuous exposure–may include areas where no billboards exist • captive audience with little else to do • selective audience: students, office workers, shoppers	• a lot of competition from other ads • only available where public transit exists • advertising material must be ready for installation two weeks prior to start date–i.e. limited flexibility

▲

Exterior bus posters are
advertisements that appear
on the outside of buses,
either along the side or the
back.

King bus posters are
located on the sides of
transit vehicles. They are
made of two pieces, held in
a metal frame.

▼

Seventy bus posters, so called because they measure 70″ × 21″, are located on the side or back of a bus. They can feature a channel insert, a special insert that enables a company to exploit special deals while retaining the main part of the advertisement.

Another exterior used to grab the attention of motorists and pedestrians is the Total Paint. For one price, Trans Ad will turn an entire bus into a moving billboard. Included in the cost of a Total Paint is all the interior transit card space.

Transit cards come in various sizes, depending on the transit system. Given that the average bus or subway trip takes nearly one-half hour, that's a lot of time during which riders have little to do except look at ads!

In those cities with either a subway (Toronto and Montreal), Light Rapid Transit (Calgary, Edmonton and Toronto), or in Vancouver with its Automated Light Rapid Transit Skytrain, Trans Ad offers a variety of products.

34

Ad Info:
1. Name the major advertising media.
2. What is prime time for television viewing in your household?
3. What are ratings?
4. What are the main types of newspaper advertising?
5. What are the various kinds of outdoor advertising?

Ad Data:
1. Based on your television viewing, how would you divide the broadcasting day?
2. If a company wanted its advertising to be seen by the following groups, which daypart would you recommend it select?
- teenagers
- office workers
- pre-school children
- retired, well-to-do senior citizens
3. Does your area have a transit system? If so, can you remember five transit ads you have seen in the last week? Write them down and compare your recollection with your class. What conclusions can you draw about the effectiveness of transit advertising to high school students?
4. Watch one TV show tonight. First record the following:
    a) the name of the show
    b) the type of people you think are most likely viewers
Then, during each commercial break, keep a count of the number of commercials by type of product or service. It would be helpful to have ready a chart similar to the one below and simply keep track by placing a check mark in the appropriate column.

At the end of the show, determine which products or services were advertised more frequently than others. Did the advertisers spend their money wisely? Base your answer on the target audience you feel the advertiser was trying to reach.
5. What effective uses of sight, sound, motion, and emotion have you seen in recent TV commercials?

candy/snack food	travel	automobile	alcohol

6. According to the outdoor advertising company Mediacom, the products on which most poster advertising dollars are spent, in order: consumer packaged goods, automobiles, clothing. Divide the area around your school. Assign each area to two people who will conduct a survey. Note the number of billboards and the products advertised. Classify them by type of product. Bring this information to class. What did you discover? What goods and services are most frequently advertised on billboards in your area? What products and services do you think are best advertised on posters?

7. Explain why you would or would not recommend television commercials for advertising the following products and services:

- a new automobile from General Motors
- a local dry cleaner
- lockers for installation in high schools
- a new fragrance from Fabergé
- a new teen club in your area
- *TV Guide* magazine

Ad Write:

1. What is your favourite magazine? Pick five products or services you think should be advertised in your choice. Write a paragraph explaining why. Don't forget to consider the strengths and weaknesses of magazine advertising in your explanation!

2. In a sentence for each, explain why you would or would not use newspapers to advertise the following:

- a garage sale
- the opening of a new store in your area
- a new brand of soft drink
- the newest release of an album by your favourite group
- a seat sale on airline flights to winter resorts
- a movie to be shown on television for the first time

3. Quickly write down a brief description of the first five television commercials that come to mind. Compare this list to your classmates'. Are there any similarities and differences? What conclusions can you draw from this information?

4. a) Suppose you are starting your own business. Pick a product or service for your business. Prepare a fact sheet for your ad agency. On it you should indicate:

- your product or service
- your target market
- most important point you want the consumer to remember about your product/service

b) Exchange fact sheets with a partner. Study the fact sheet and make a recommendation as to the medium (media) in which your partner should advertise. Provide three basic ideas or approaches showing how you would design the ad if you were awarded the contract. ■

THE ADVERTISING AGENCY

Some advertisers, particularly the smallest, decide on the medium to use and the message to deliver without any outside help. Most large and small companies and organizations, however, use advertising agencies to help make these decisions.

An advertising agency works with its **client** (the advertiser) to develop an effective advertising campaign. The full-service agency, working with the client, then creates, produces, and places the advertising. Some advertising agencies are **limited service** agencies. Limited service agencies do not offer all services, but specialize in certain areas such as creating ads, buying advertising time and space. Limited service agencies do work for companies that do some of their own advertising, and for other agencies.

Computers have made creating advertising quicker and easier. Many advertisers still use the services of a full-service agency, however, to meet their advertising needs. In addition to designing and creating ads and producing commercials, full-service agencies offer marketing research, as well as advertising space in newspapers and magazines, and radio and television time. Full-service agencies are divided into four major departments:

- client services
- creative
- media
- research

Client services co-ordinates the business relationship between the agency and the client. Each client is assigned an **account executive** who is responsible for dealing day-to-day with the client, and spends a great deal of time analysing information about the client's business (e.g. market share, competition, marketing research information and so on). This helps the client develop the advertising and aids the client's other marketing activities.

Meet an Account Executive

John Clarke, who is in his early twenties, is one of the youngest members in the Toronto office of the international advertising agency, D'Arcy Masius Benton & Bowles (DMB&B). DMB&B is a long established agency with a variety of clients, including Procter & Gamble, Effem Foods, and Labatt's.

When he finished university, John could have taken a position in another area of business that was initially more financially rewarding. However, he wanted to be in advertising. John knew that to start in advertising without previous experience, it would be necessary to work his way up from an entry-level position. Therefore, he started in the media department. John first worked in the media department of another agency. Although it involved long hours for modest pay, he gained a good deal of knowledge about the different advertising media and the various aspects of agency work. Because he was dedicated, he gained some recognition in the advertising business and was able to continue on and join client services at DMB&B.

John says it is still possible to get into advertising without having a university degree. He suggests that a degree in advertising from a community college can serve as a good starting point for those of you seeking a career in advertising. Whichever path you take, if you have the ambition and drive to succeed, you will quickly climb.

Ad Note

An account executive requires organizational skills, the ability to work with a variety of people, including: peers, subordinates, superiors, clients and creative people. Most account executives have university degrees.

The **creative department** is responsible for the actual creation and production of the ads. Working with the client, the creative department and client services work through the ideas that become an advertisement or commercial. The process of actually creating an ad varies from agency to agency. At some it is a team effort with many people involved. At others it may be one **copywriter** and an **art director** who discuss the words and the illustration.

Ad Note

A copywriter must be able to write for many different target markets. Copywriters spend hours writing and re-writing just to get the right mix of words and ideas. An art director is responsible for the appearance of the ad — the typeface used, the illustration, the size of the ad, and so on. Most have some artistic talent that has been developed at a college of art.

The creative department is also responsible for producing ads and commercials. Sometimes the actual production of the commercial is handled by an outside company. In either case, organizing and setting up a commercial is a time-consuming task. For example, Animation House, a Canadian company that produces television commercials, may take as many as five months to produce one of its commercials, using animated clay figures.

The **media department** is responsible for the planning, purchasing, and scheduling of advertising time and space. The department recommends where, when, and how much advertising to place, based on the client's plan and requirements. Once a plan is approved, it must be purchased from the various media representatives. Preparing and purchasing media requires negotiation and planning skills, since advertising time and space is often booked months, sometimes as much as a year in advance. In addition, people in media must know the strengths, weaknesses, and costs of the various media throughout the country. Fortunately, much of this information is now computerized.

Ad Note

The media department is often the entry-level position for people who wish to start their careers in advertising. The successful person can grow with the position and the company to take on additional responsibilities in media, or move to other areas of the agency.

This commercial for
TransAlta Utilities was
painstakingly produced
using frame after frame of
clay figures.

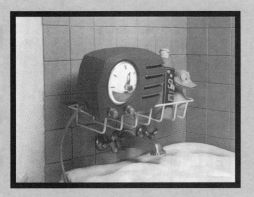 

 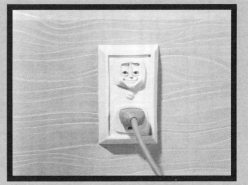

The **research department** provides the basic marketing information used in developing the
advertising. A research department works with clients to
develop a research plan, collects
and analyses the data, and reports
to the client. Researchers may
investigate the size of the market
for a new product proposed by the
client, analyse the success of a
sales promotion, or research the
effectiveness of the advertising a
company is using or plans to use.

Creating Advertising

Look back at the two ads on page
8. What was your reaction to
them? Have you seen them else-
where? Did they attract your
attention? Have you purchased
any of the products they advertise? If you answered "yes" to the
above questions, the advertisers
used the AIDA formula successfully. The AIDA formula is common to all good advertising. AIDA
stands for:

A attention

I interest

D desire

A action

Attention

Put simply, an ad that does not
attract your attention cannot be
effective. If a television commercial does not capture attention, it
is likely to be "zapped." If a print
ad does not catch your eye, the
reader turns the page.

Getting and keeping attention is
difficult. Recent research has discovered that on average, only four
out of every one hundred ads are
remembered the next day! A
magazine ad has less than one-half
second to capture and hold the
reader's attention!

There are many ways advertisers can try to capture attention.
For example, radio advertising
uses music and sound effects.
Print and television advertisers
use colour. Colour presents a realism that is difficult or impossible
to portray in black and white. Try
to imagine McDonald's commercials in black and white! Colours
also carry a meaning. Black and
gold are luxurious colours, often
seen in advertisements for jewel-
lery. Blues and greens are cool colours representing spring time,
the sky, or water. Green is particularly effective in telling soft drink
consumers that the advertised
product is refreshing. Yellow, of
course, is the colour of sunshine.
You would expect to see yellow in
an ad for winter travel to a warm
weather resort, or in a sunscreen
ad.

Black and white, however, can
be used effectively in magazines
and on television where colour is
normally used. Because ads in
black and white are different and
unexpected, they can capture
attention.

In television advertising, colour, along with sound, motion,
and volume changes, is used to

attract attention. Pepsi often uses celebrities from the music industry in its advertising. The music and the celebrity, along with the lights and other special effects, attract attention.

Newspaper, magazine, transit, and poster advertising use the **headline** and/or the **illustration** (picture) to get attention. A successful headline or illustration may use such techniques as shock effect, or images that don't seem to fit the copy on the product, in order to get attention.

Another method advertisers use to attract attention in all media is the appearance of a well-known person in the ad. This is called **testimonial** or **endorsement** advertising. Well-known actors, actresses, and sports figures often appear in such advertisements.

Using a celebrity is not, however, a guarantee of success. Actress Grace Jones's television commercials for Honda motorcycles did not improve sales. Pepsi's two minute commercial starring Madonna generated controversy because a racy rock video by the singer appeared at roughly the same time. The commercial was quickly taken off the air. The person giving the testimonial need not be "real." An actor wearing a stethoscope, or standing in a laboratory can play the part of a scientist or doctor recommending a product.

The testimonial can also be given by a non-human character. Morris the Cat has been the "spokescat" for Nine Lives cat food for many years. (By the way, the first Morris is no longer with us.)

Interest

Getting attention is not enough. After getting attention, an ad must hold the interest of the audience. When someone sees or hears an ad, that person thinks, "What's in it for me?" If the ad doesn't answer this question, consumers won't keep reading, or listening, or watching. Consumers are interested in how the advertised product or service meets their wants and needs. An effective ad describes how the product or service will satisfy the consumers' wants and needs.

Creating interest is a challenge of preparing good advertising. Many ads get attention, but not all effectively generate interest. One reason for this may be that the ad discusses the product's features, rather than how the consumer will benefit. Look at the following ad.

Would consumers be interested if Mr. Clean were simply advertised as a smooth, thick cream, rather than a liquid or powdered cleanser, without having the "tough on dirt," "soft on surfaces" benefits made clear to them? An ad must also communicate a benefit that consumers find important. For example, disposable diapers were only mildly successful when marketed as being more convenient than cloth diapers. Sales really grew when the benefit advertised was the product keeping babies drier. Happier babies meant a real benefit for new parents.

Another way advertisers create interest is by suggesting there is a secret only users of the product or service know. Everybody loves a secret. The following advertisement generated a great deal of interest.

Advertisers often use young children in ads. Little kids are "cute." Ads containing children are often "heartwarming." So advertisers play on emotions that make us vulnerable to their appeals. One technique which works especially well generating interest is humour.

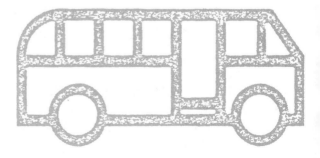

These ads for Saab work well both at the emotional and intellectual levels.

Some observers have noted disturbing trends in current advertising. Read the following article to find out these trends and the basic emotion to which they appeal.

The World According to Commercials

BY GREG QUILL TORONTO STAR

It's a jungle out there.

If you doubt it, just look at the way a growing number of TV advertisers are using mini-dramas, even domestic tragedies, to pitch their products and services.

Not as better, bigger, stronger, less expensive, longer lasting, more efficient or simply more fun than the competition, mind you, but as the necessary stuff of life in the cruel and callous late 1980s, crucial to our well-being, to our survival.

In an American-made TV commercial for British Airways, a group of lean and hungry corporate wolves in a London boardroom are seen congratulating themselves on having devised a plot to embarrass and perhaps overthrow another member of their organization. He's due at an early morning meeting, having flown all night from New York, they think, on a no-frills, red-eye flight they've booked for him. They resent his returning from New York "thinking he knows everything."

What *they* don't know is that the homecoming executive has changed airlines. For the same price, it's pre-sumed, (company expense accounts are sacred these days), he's taken a British Airways flight and has been pampered with food and drink, and allowed to work and rest peacefully. To the obvious chagrin of the snake-eyed plotters, our hero arrives for the meeting on time — refreshed, prepared and in control.

British Airways has helped avert a corporate coup.

That commercial is a long way in tone — but not far in psychological impact — from the Bell Canada ad in which the genial, only slightly despotic grapple grommet manufacturer (played with stunning cunning by Toronto actor Larry Mann) leads his apparently brain-dead underlings into an airport lounge before setting off on a business trip.

Call ahead

But instead of allowing them a five-minute breather before the flight, the boss urges his drones to "call ahead" from the lounge phones to clients in other cities, or "back to the office to tie up loose ends."

They all, of course, oblige, like so many intimidated slaves, behind Mann's condescending sneer.

In another American-made TV commercial, for the AT&T telecommunications company, an executive bumps into a couple of business colleagues — over what appears to be a breakfast meeting, no less — closing a real estate deal with a competitor.

He had bid on the property, too, the executive says, shocked and angry. He should have been allowed a counter offer.

"We left a message at your office last night," the kind, concerned seller replies.

The executive's face falls, his pupils even seem to contract with fear, a shadow of a tremor flickers across his lower lip.

"You left a *message* . . . ?"

And with the sudden, grotesque realization that his telephone system is imperfect, the only sound the executive hears resembles the slamming of a prison door, or perhaps the falling of a gallows trap.

At the very least, his career is in the dumper.

Good grief! What's going on here? Have we reached such a low creative ebb in the decline of the Decade Of Don't (as in drink, have sex, smoke, eat meat, take drugs, trust anyone, gain weight, buck the system, let them see you sweat, express an opinion, make a mistake, be late, park without a permit, turn left before 6.30 p.m., walk the dog without a leash and a scoop) that we have to convince people their livelihoods and the welfare of their families depend on which brand of telephone they use — or whether they use one often enough?

Grim world

Is the business world so grim that snakes-in-the-boardroom, people who work for the same organization yet connive against each other, have become commonplace, mere props to sell a new class of air travel?

Are we really meant to believe — as American Express would have it — that, unless we have a no-limit credit card that enables us to buy first-class plane tickets when economy flights are full and rent limousines when there are no taxis, we'll risk being late and disappointing our children?

That's what this new trend in advertising amounts to: selling by fear. In these modern mini-morality plays, these nightmares of the upwardly mobile, our lives are perpetually in the balance, and only products can restore equilibrium.

The messages we're getting aren't appealing at all. We're learning to feel even more insecure, that co-workers are plotting to get our jobs, because we're smart alecs, that our bosses think we're simpletons at best and, at worst, entirely dispensable, unless we fulfill their every whim.

We're coming to understand that the lack of a credit card could cost us the love of our children, and that a missed phone message could cost us our careers . . . or our necks.

And that without the *Yellow Pages*, whose benefits are depicted in a strangely anachronistic, postwar-era TV commercial featuring an old, worried mother and an impossibly cute red-headed boy who can't get work, we might *never* find a job. Worse, if you take stock of the way the mother and son are dressed and the furnishings in their meagre hovel, there's a more sinister message: Without the *Yellow Pages*, without a job, we might all be living in 1946 . . . in a ghetto . . . in the rain . . . in sepia tones.

Brutal copies

That's scary.

But the new go-for-the-throat realism in advertising, even the brutal and the intimidating, suits advertisers just fine, says Gail Wasserman, of the New York advertising company Ogilivy & Mather, which developed the AT & T commercials and is somewhat proud of having started the trend.

There are all sorts of imitations now,'' she said earlier this week. "I saw one the other day where an insurance company showed a family being destroyed because financial matters weren't properly taken care of.

''They don't make people who watch them feel great,'' she added. ''They produce anxiety, worry. But most people also recognize they represent the reality of a competitive business world.

''And they get great results for our clients.''

Mastermind of the new reality in advertising is Ogilvy & Mather's creative director, John Doig, who set out a year ago to counter what he recently called the ''Genetic creature in advertising, with the perfect teeth, who never gets pimples, who speaks in a language bred for TV commercials.

With the breakfast meeting ad—and another series in which small business people talk quietly about how their lives and livelihoods were destroyed by inadequate telecommunications systems—Doig said he wanted ''to create a sense of unease. It's a little bit like looking through a keyhole.''

Genuine situations

To complete his vision, Doig hired documentary moviemaker John Nathan, whose use of handheld cameras, extreme close-ups and close microphones (no one shouts in these commercials) enhance the sense of real panic that emerges from copywriter Marc Welsh's tense, terse scripts, themselves based on real business scenarios and genuine dialogue.

The commercials, like most of their imitators, were shot in genuine business situations, in office buildings and work areas, using available light and ordinary-looking stage actors without make-up. The effect is chilling. And the campaign is so successful in the U.S. that it will likely be duplicated in AT&T's Canadian TV campaign in January, says Don Tanguay, Ogilvy & Mather Canada's director of marketing services.

''The trend certainly exists and I see no reason wny we wouldn't adapt the U.S. material.''

Oh, great. Now even advertising companies have given up on fantasy. In a world where ordinary people are beset by unprecedented economic hardship, by social and political horrors, by dwindling moral values and laws too complex to bear, commercial makers have found that holding up a mirror can shock us into buying stuff like we've never bought stuff before.

But not for the old reasons, not to feel pretty or clean or satisfied. We're buying now for self-protection, because we're frightened for our jobs and our families. We're hunkering down, looking after No. 1, digging in — ugly as that sounds.

At least, that's what it looks like on TV. ∎

Fear has been used to some extent for a long time. Consider advertisements for personal care products. Ads for mouthwashes, breath mints, and deodorants have long played on our concern about being socially acceptable.

The appeal to fear has been used to good effect in some advertising. Look at the following ad.

In this case, the advertisement is a reminder that a painful death can occur as a result of smoking — surely a more legitimate reason for being fearful than having bad breath or cavities!

Sometimes advertisers sell the consumer a desirable image along with the product. Read what this journalist has to say about such advertising.

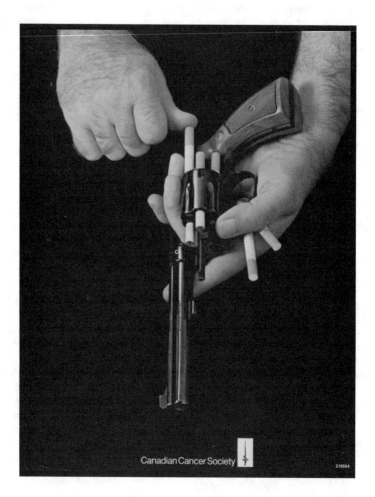

Canadian Cancer Society

What advertising and image can do

Few people buy a perfume advertised as "a lovely blend of deer-gland secretions, alcohol, and pine resin." But they would buy a scent that promises to attract the opposite sex, or make them feel glamorous, mysterious, exotic, or successful. These are just a few of the lures that perfume ads dangle in front of us. While consumers know that perfume can't really change their appearance or personality, they want to believe it anyway. And so, the image and advertising of a fragrance is an important selling point — perhaps more important than its scent. In fact, according to The Fragrance Foundation, psychological testing indicates that a fragrance's name, package, and advertising — everything that makes up its image — not only influence how we perceive the scent, but actually contribute to the total sensory experience.

Experts agree that advertising should be designed to prepare the buyer for the pleasure he or she will obtain when using the fragrance. They believe that the perfume must make the user feel the emotional pleasures of romance, love, health and fitness, youth, happiness, fashion, music, and exotic or artistic places. All the elements of the perfume — scent, name, bottle, label, package, and advertising — must combine in harmony to create a special image in the mind of the consumer.

Does the creation of an image sell perfume? You bet! So much so, that consumers usually fall in love with the image of a fragrance before they fall in love with the scent itself. And manufacturers are banking on that. They know that on first sniff, you either like or dislike the stuff and there's nothing they can do about that. But if they can create a positive image for a fragrance, they know they can actually influence how you feel about that all-important first sniff. And that can influence you to buy a fragrance that you may have otherwise decided wasn't for you.

Take Ralph Lauren's Chaps for instance. A recent article in *Vogue* told this true story. "Ralph Lauren's Chaps was launched in 1979 with a strong cowboy image, an image its sellers considered to represent independence, ruggedness, pride in American heritage, a free spirit. As sales slowed, studies revealed that American attitudes had changed. Women (buyers of 80 percent of men's fragrances) perceived the cowboy as a lone figure, too macho, and self-contained. Men had a status problem with it and felt that the cowboy worked the ranch while the man in the Stetson Cologne ad owned it.'' As a result, ''Chaps's revised — and most successful — commercial to date is a switch from the cowboy image to an outdoorsy modern man shown with a woman and children and with others whom he cares about and who care about him. The message: What appeals today is not macho, but the attractiveness of a fit, active man who takes care of himself.'' Proof positive that image and advertising can make or break a fragrance.

Let's look at a perfume advertisement that is currently running on TV. It'll show you how advertisements create an image for a scent and tempt you to buy.

In this ad you see a beautiful girl with long flowing blonde hair. She's wearing a long flowing white dress and riding a shining white horse across a meadow of flowers. Everything is in soft focus — as if she is living in a dream world. What do you think that ad is trying to tell you? Well, for one thing it's telling you that this girl is happy, and her life is carefree — as if she were living in a dream world.

Let's go back to the ad. Now, you see the girl spraying herself with a particular perfume — and then a guy appears and gives her a kiss. What the ad is trying to tell you now is that if you use this perfume you'll be just like this girl. Your life will be free and easy, and you'll attract a boyfriend, too. But is that true? No, of course not. Your ability to have a happy life and attract a boyfriend can only come from inside you and not from inside a perfume bottle.

So, what's wrong with buying an image? Absolute nothing . . . as long as you're aware that image is a big part of what you're paying for. And as long as you don't get fooled into thinking that wearing a fragrance can change you or your life. ■

Desire

Getting attention and holding interest are only part of AIDA. Advertising must generate a desire to either learn more about the product or service or a desire to acquire it. One way advertisers generate consumers' desire is by showing others enjoying the product or service. In travel advertising, showing people on the beach enjoying themselves is a way to generate the desire to travel.

Putting You In The Picture Is Paramount

MEXICO · CARIBBEAN · HAWAII · BERMUDA
FLORIDA · CRUISING

Paramount
H·O·L·I·D·A·Y·S

Food or restaurant
advertising generates
desire by showing the food
in appetizing photographs,
or being consumed.

THE ESSENCE OF STYLE

To experience
SUNG...
Open the fold
and stroke the
scented strip
on the inside
of your wrist.

SUNG

RFUM   ALFRED SUNG   EAU DE TOILETTE

the Bay

A scented magazine insert
is another way advertisers
stimulate the consumers'
desire to purchase.

Action

At this point, if the advertiser has successfully attracted attention, created interest, and stimulated desire, the consumer will be thinking, "I want to purchase." If the ad does not give the consumer the information needed to obtain the product, however, then the advertising is wasted. An ad must give the consumer an opportunity to take some sort of action. Good advertising often concludes with a message or information that tells the consumer what to do next. Examples include; "Call this toll-free number today for details," "Don't delay," "Buy now before it is too late," "See your travel agent or call Air Canada today," "Return the enclosed card immediately." The advertiser might simply tell consumers where the product is available.

Some print ads include a coupon as part of the advertisement. This is another way to encourage the consumer to take action and purchase the product or service.

The following ad illustrates each part of the AIDA formula.

The headline gets **attention**. Abrupt alliterative caption leads reader on by forcing a response to the implied question: What is short and sweet? The ad keeps **interest** by offering tempting and healthy recipes. **Desire** is prompted by the luscious-looking and larger than life illustration. Most importantly, the ad leads to **action** by giving Foodland Ontario's address and telephone number, so that readers can easily find out the nearest strawberry patch.

Ad Info:

1. What does an advertising agency do?
2. a) What is the role of client services in an advertising agency?
   b) What does the creative department of an advertising agency do?
   c) What does the media department do?
   d) What is the role of the research department?
   e) In which of the four departments would you prefer to work and why?
3. What does AIDA stand for?
4. What is testimonial advertising? In addition to attracting attention, what might it accomplish?
5. In both of these ads, find one feature and one benefit.

Ad Data:

1. Either in class or at home, listen to five radio ads. How did the advertiser use sound to get attention? Develop a database from the survey you made of these commercials.

2. Television uses colour, sound, motion, and volume changes in order to get attention. Which method most effectively gets your attention? which least effectively? How do your opinions compare with those of others in your class?

3. Working in a group, find at least one ad from each medium that uses a well-known person. What kinds of products and services do they advertise? Discuss why you think each personality was chosen for the particular product or service.

4. Reread the article on p. 49. What is your opinion of the techniques it describes? Discuss why fear is effective in advertising. Do you think such advertising should be allowed? Why or why not?

5. Look at the ads you have collected so far, or at a newspaper or magazine. How many advertisers use emotion to get interest? Which emotions are used?

6. Choose two print advertisements. Circle the parts that attract your attention, build your interest, arouse your desire, and suggest or inspire you to action.

Ad Write:

1. Which of the following would you suggest be used in an ad or commercial for a product or service targeted to males and females 13–20 years of age? Justify your choices. Also explain why you feel the others would not be effective.

- babies
- animals
- cars
- a beach
- food
- cartoon characters

Pick one item from the above list and, using this, prepare a print ad for a product or service and target market of your choice. When the ads are complete, exchange with a partner and see if you can suggest any improvement to each other's ad.

2. Reread the article on p. 53. What is your opinion of the last paragraph? Is it always easy to tell when advertisers are offering an image? Rework the ad you created for question 1. Develop it so that it sells an image. What kinds of images would work best with your target market?

PREPARING ADVERTISING

Now that you have an idea of how advertisers use the AIDA formula, let's look at what's involved in preparing advertising for the various media.

Print Advertising

Newspaper and magazine advertising start with the **layout**. The layout shows the arrangement of the ad.

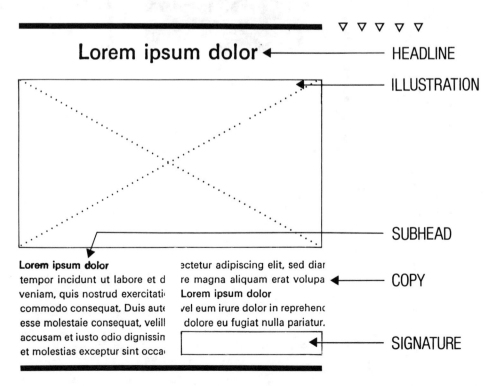

▽ ▽ ▽ ▽ ▽

Lorem ipsum dolor ◄——————— HEADLINE

◄——————— ILLUSTRATION

◄——————— SUBHEAD

Lorem ipsum dolor
tempor incidunt ut labore et d   ectetur adipiscing elit, sed diar
veniam, quis nostrud exercitati   re magna aliquam erat volupa ◄——————— COPY
commodo consequat. Duis aute   **Lorem ipsum dolor**
esse molestaie consequat, velill vel eum irure dolor in reprehenc
accusam et iusto odio dignissin   dolore eu fugiat nulla pariatur.
et molestias exceptur sint occa

◄——————— SIGNATURE

As you have discovered, a **headline** can be the key to attracting attention. Because many readers read only the headline, it should stop the reader from flipping past the ad by offering a benefit, stating a fact that demands the reader's attention, or by shocking the reader to attention.

Advertisers use a variety of headline types. The name of the product or service appears prom-
inently

Coke is It!
New Breck concentrate
Shampoo

The headline is a command

Help Stamp Out Runny
Noses
Meet you at the Bay!

The headline is a question

Why Buy At Towers?
How Can Just 1 Calorie
Taste So Good?
What Price Success?

The headline states a benefit

The greatest sale in our
history
There has never been a
better time to buy
World-proven performance

The headline makes a claim

For Immediate Relief
Cars for People Without
Cars
The Fastest Way to Fly Free

The headline makes a personal-
ized statement

When Your Children Stop
Asking Questions, Start
Worrying

In addition to the headline, many ads contain **subheads**. These are mini-headlines that appear lower in the ad. Subheads break up the print, making the copy easier to read. Subheads also make the ad more appealing and help direct the reader's eyes to important facts.

Most print ads also include an **illustration**, a photograph or drawing in black and white, or colour, which often highlights user benefits by showing the product or service in a number of different ways. For instance, an automobile can be shown as a family vehicle if children are placed in the picture. Or, the auto could be shown alone, as an appeal to sporty tastes, or prestige of the buyer. The car could be photographed travelling the autobahn, or racing along Le Mans roads. This is the appeal of the exciting location.

In some ads, the illustration is the major element of the ad. Little else is included.

Copy is the written part of an ad. Copy usually explains the features and benefits of the product or service being advertised. The copy should turn the reader's interest into desire, and include the information needed to take action. Good copy has four main characteristics; it is:

- direct
- imaginative
- to the point
- readable

Good copy is written as if a potential consumer remarks; "I am thinking of taking a trip, [or buying a stereo, etc.]. Which would you recommend and why?" and a copywriter responds with a newly created ad.

No one forces people to read an ad. If the copy becomes boring, the reader flips the page. To keep interest and arouse desire for the product or service, copy must use words in a way that keeps the reader interested.

Consumers will not spend much time reading the copy to find the key parts of the advertisement. Therefore, good copy gets right to the point. One example of straightforward copy is the following. It was written in the early 1900s by the Arctic explorer Ernest Shackleton when he recruited men for an Arctic expedition.

> **Men wanted for hazardous journey. Small wages, bitter cold, long months of complete darkness, constant danger, safe return doubtful. Honour and recognition in case of success.**

Getting to the point, however, doesn't necessarily mean the copy is short. If the product has many good qualities, is expensive or technical, then long copy is acceptable and necessary.

If the product is widely known and used, such as soap, long copy would be unnecessary and boring to read.

Copy should be written so that the target market understands the meaning. If the target market consists of doctors, for example, there is nothing wrong with using technical words. If the target market is consumers from many walks of life, however, the copy must use words common in day-to-day conversation.

Many ads conclude with a **signature** which indicates who sells the product or service, or where to go to purchase it. This is the action part of the AIDA formula. The signature includes information the consumer needs to act. Such information might include the address or telephone number.

71

Radio Advertising

A radio ad starts out like a movie — with a **script**. The script includes all the words and instructions for the sound effects and music. The script can then be read live or taped for rebroadcast.

Little Girl
Child:

Yesterday, we were supposed to visit grandma. But mom and dad said they had more important things to do. When I asked why we didn't go, mom said shopping was more important. Dad said he didn't feel like driving all that way. I remember the last time we were there. She was in her room all alone staring out the window at the rain. Grandma says she likes the rain. I like my grandma. Sometimes she gives me candy from her secret hiding place. I wish I could hug her right now.

Announcer:

The elderly. They'd really appreciate a call or a caring hand. A message from the broadcasters of B.C. and University Hospital at three sites, Shaughnessy, UBC and George Derby Centre. We care about caring for the aged, wherever they are in B.C.

The following chart shows the four main types of scripts: announcement, testimonial, dialogue, and musical.

Types of Scripts

announcement	Information about the product or service is read to the audience by an announcer. Such ads are often read on the air between sets of music.
testimonial	As in print advertising, radio advertisers use a celebrity to endorse the product or service because it improves the credibility of the message.
dialogue	The ad is presented as a story or conversation between two or more people. It can be humorous or serious.
musical	The script includes a great deal of music or a jingle to get your attention and keep interest.

One key to writing radio advertising is making sure that the message will get across to the target market in the time allowed. Most radio ads are 30 or 60 seconds long. This is only 60 or 100 words. Therefore, radio advertising should be short and to the point. Because radio lacks the visual element, the best commercials inspire the listener's imagination. Another way radio advertisers make up for the lack of a visual element is by frequently repeating the name of the product or a telephone number in order to emphasize it. Repetition ensures that the company or product name is not only heard, but remembered after the commercial is over.

The human voice on the radio effects the intimacy of the one-to-one contact of a personal sales call. The voice used should match the message and fit the product. If the product is one that is tough on acne blemishes, the voice used should sound tough!

Television Advertising

Because of the visual component, television advertising is much more complicated, time-consuming, and expensive to produce than other forms of advertising. These difficulties also make creating television commercials challenging and exciting.

The types of television commercials are very similar to those used in the other media. Announcements and testimonials are often used. Slice of life is used in radio and in the print media, but because television allows the advertiser to use sight and motion, as well as sound, it works particularly well in television.

Slice of life is a "mini-drama." First you see a person with a problem. Next, a person with the solution to the problem (the product) arrives. The product is then used to solve the problem. Thus we see people whose lives appear blighted by dirty laundry, grubby floors, dusty furniture, and other problems too numerous to mention. All of them have their problem solved and their lives apparently transformed by the advertiser's product. The commercial finishes with a happy ending.

Television is the only medium that allows the advertiser to demonstrate the product or service being used. Automobile commercials often demonstrate the vehicle climbing a hill, or negotiating pylons on a test track, or pulling up in front of a luxurious restaurant. Diaper commercials show how one diaper absorbs water better than another.

After deciding which type of commercial to produce, and before starting to film it, the advertising agency prepares a **storyboard**. A storyboard is a rough draft of the commercial drawn on paper. There are two types. A **rough board** is used by the advertising agency in preparing the ad. It is not formally presented to the client. It includes each element of the commercial side-by-side.

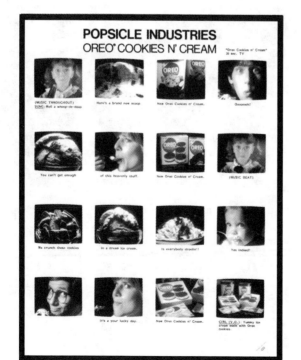

When the commercial is ready to be presented to the client, a **comprehensive storyboard** is created. The images are drawn by an artist. Beneath each picture are the dialogue and any shooting instructions for the director. This board is then used by the advertising agency to sell the commercial to the advertiser. If approved, the comprehensive storyboard becomes the production guide for the commercial.

In case you think, at this point, that making a TV commercial is a fairly cut-and-dried procedure, the foregoing has provided you with only the bare bones. Read the following article which "tells it like it is."

Ad Note

Technology is creating a new set of problems for television advertisers. Television commercials are under attack by new creatures of the electronic age: **zappers**, **muters**, **zippers** and **flippers**. These are names for people who do various things to commercials with either a VCR or a remote-control channel selector. **Flippers** are those people who use their channel changer to randomly flip from program to program. Some people **zap** past commercials with channel changers, or **mute** the sound when the commericals come on. Others use the fast forward feature to **zip** by the commercials on programs recorded on VCRs.

Commercial avoidance can be a big problem for television advertisers. For example, a study found that the household that made the most "zaps" changed channels over 1000 times during a day! As a result, commercials are getting shorter; 15 second commercials are becoming more popular. The next step may be the eight second ad. Pepsi recently used this format in Paris. Television viewers like them because they don't take up much time. Advertisers like shorter commercials not only because they are less expensive, but also because they are difficult to zap, mute, zip, or flip.

How to make a TV commercial

BY DAVE CHENOWETH THE GAZETTE

Thirty seconds: For most of us, that's no time at all.

Yet television commercials take only 30 seconds to create an entire mini-universe, complete with plot, characters, humour, conflict. Those 30 seconds must not only capture our attention but — unlike a novel or movie — actually encourage us to *do something*.

Every day on television, dozens of these "30-second theatres" reach out to millions of viewers. Each ad can represent hundreds of hours of work and cost thousands of dollars.

Take the 30-second spot promoting men's apparel from Montreal's Merit Clothing. Right now audiences are catching it from Ontario to the West Coast. Here in Montreal you can see it via cable on CJOH.

The Merit spot was put together by the local office of J. Walter Thompson — the world's largest advertising agency, best known as JWT — and produced by Toronto's Aisha Film Co.

Three vignettes

It contains three vignettes of well-dressed heroes receiving admiring glances from women and envious glances from men. Two men leave a squash club; a corporate executive attends a business meeting; a man meets friends for lunch. The tagline at the end sums up: "Merit: The look that gets the looks."

Take one: Planning. The first steps in an ad like Merit's are taken long before a single foot of film is shot. For Merit, it began last spring, when the company switched its advertising account to JWT.

First came meetings between the Merit marketing executives and JWT's account director Wendell Pope and account supervisor Jane Williams.

Together they hammered out Merit's basic marketing goals: To appeal to men between 29 and 45 years old; and to project that Merit clothes combine both quality and with-it fashion in a wide range of styles.

Applying the marketing strategies is the job of the agency's creative department. Merit's ad is scripted by vice-president and creative director Marlene Hore, a miniature dynamo.

Target group

"The client has defined a target group, the people he wanted to talk to — and this comes from a whole lot of analysis on his market situation." Hore explains. "Then I take all this info and digest it and put it together — and arrive at a piece of paper which is in fact the script.

"Then we present this to the client, who either buys it or rejects it, and eventually we arrive at a commercial."

In the case of Merit, the vignettes in the ad demonstrate the range of Merit clothes; she also scripts to match the strategy: "A Merit suit will make a man look his best, enhancing his self-confidence and, therefore, making him appear successful and attractive to other people."

Take Two: The Production House. Once the ad has been approved by the client, the agency selects an outside production house that will actually film the ad. It briefs the production house crew — essentially a producer and a director — on what will be needed.

Hore says there are 15 or 20 top-level production houses in Canada. "Each of them can have certain strengths: Some have a strong bent for humour, some are best for ads that require pretty pictures, some are better than others at working with big-name stars. We pick a few that are good in the area we want for a certain ad, and ask them to submit quotes."

But money is far from the deciding factor:

"A script is just a script: every director will leave his mark on the commercial, he's definitely part of the creative process."

The production house selected for the Merit ad is Toronto's Aisha Films — a new company, but one whose partners have worked with the JWT people before. One of the strengths of Aisha is partner Ousama Rawi, who will direct the shoot: As well as having worked in commercials for over 15 years in Britain and Canada, he's also a successful feature-film cinematographer. He was a cameraman on the Michael Caine movie *Pulp* and such Canadian films as *Power Play*.

Although 'Ossie' Rawi is reluctant to discuss his fees, he does say that novice commercial directors can earn between $700-$800 a day; an experienced man can demand as high as $2500 for a day's shooting — "it all depends on how much weight he carries."

Once a production house has been selected, further discussions take place, as client representatives, the agency people and the production house seniors work out the details of the ad, and especially the budget details.

The cost of a 30-second spot ranges up from the low thousands — for just a "talking head" as an announcer declaims the merits of a product — to the six-figure bracket, depending on whether the ad includes big-name stars, exotic locations or demanding special effects.

The Merit ad will cost in the range of $40 000.

• $25 000 goes for production house fees, director Rawi, equipment and crew, plus editing costs

• $5000 or so goes for 'talent' — main performers plus background extras.

•Another $5000 goes for a music track, with travel expenses and other minor details adding another couple of thousand.

Take Three: The Casting Session. It is a sweltering afternoon. Even two straining fans can't keep the temperature under 80 degrees in the big meeting room at Aisha Films.

Nobody looks comfortable: Not the half-dozen agency and production house people sitting around the glass-topped table. Not the 60-odd models and actors — handsome men and lovely women vying for the lead roles, a scattering of older men as possible *maitres-d'* or background figures to admire the 'Merit men' — who enter two or three at a time for the minutes-brief auditions.

Formula auditions

Ossie Rawa supervises the auditions, a set formula:

"Do you have any other commercials now running? What other work have you done — stage, screen?"

To men with longish hair or mustaches: "Are you willing to get a haircut? Shave the mustache?" if that's what's needed to fit the Merit image.

At Ossie's back is a video camera, while at table-head is a television set showing the production executives how the talent looks on-screen.

The camera zooms in on each woman's eyes: Closeups of admiring eyes are important in the Merit ad. The men are asked to walk the length of the room, the camera following to see if they move with confidence and style.

When the auditions are over, the group will use the video records for a final decision.

The agency's women have expressed more than passing approval for some of the male models; one of the male executives has retorted with a mocking charge of "sexism."

"I don't want to hear anything about chauvinism from you guys," replies Hore.

"This is fabulous; most of the time all we get to see at these sessions are women — now it's our turn."

Irwin Ludmer, Merit's director of marketing, has a serious question — a shift from the teasing he's received for having spotted one of the auditioning models — Quebec's Sylvie Garant — (she gets the part).

He's worried that the males may look too young for the upper end of the 29-45 target group to identify with.

Account executive Jane Williams reassures him: "I don't think we have to show older men to get the viewers to associate success with what we're showing. They just can't be teenagers. Once you've got them in the right wardrobe and makeup, the shot will give them the age and dignity we need."

Take Four: The pre-production meeting. It's a week later, back in Montreal. The morning has been spent at the Metropolitan Blvd. E. offices of Merit, choosing the clothes the Merit men will wear. On the selection committee are the agency people, director Rawi, and Merit's Ludmer and executive vice-president Stanley Silverstone.

Ludmer and Silverstone want to make sure the clothes are not tied to any single season, since the ad will be used not only this fall, but next spring as well.

Silverstone isn't sure that the boardroom scene should even use a pinstripe suit: Maybe it's too traditional. Maybe the firm's retail dealers will think it's unnecessary to promote such a basic item.

In turn, director Rawi has to sort out materials that will photograph best.

And Ludmer wonders if former Montrealer Michel Gormley doesn't look out of place, too young to be the 'chairman of the board'?

Then it's a working lunch at the Mountain St. offices of JWT, complete with agenda and videotapes of the performers selected for the commercial.

Account executive Williams again details the responses the ad should evoke: "Merit is good-looking, high-quality men's clothing." This should produce an audience "belief" that "A Merit outfit will make me look attractive and successful. It's great value."

Then it's over to Aisha producer Roseanne McWaters. Arrangements are made for the models to be fitted for their on-air clothes early next week at a Merit dealer.

One problem

There are Polaroid pictures of the restaurant and athletics club that will be used as shooting locations. There is one problem: The company hasn't yet found the 'boardroom' it needs for Michel Gormley's sequence. But by next week, everything should be fine.

Director Rawi takes over now, giving a final rundown on the way the ad will be shot.

In the first sequence, we will see two Merit men leaving the squash club — the door held open for them by a man who's not dressed particularly well.

"Then the camera will be low, tracking our two guys, and there'll be a quick intercut of a pair of female legs; the legs stop dead, then we cut to the admiring eyes looking at the Merit clothes . . .''

Merit's Silverstone, one of two brothers who own the company, interjects:

"The only concern I have is with the practicality here; that what we're doing doesn't look too phoney, too sexy so that it's silly?''

"I see the legs as simply a piece of story-telling,'' replies Rawi. "If you didn't have the legs, if we just jumped from the men to the admiring eyes, you'd be completely disoriented. The layman would say: 'What the hell are eyes doing here?''

Silverstone is also concerned that the ad may be too obvious, having the men in the background look too scruffy.

Creative director Hore fields this one: "Stanley, our guys do have to be the heroes. Anyway, they won't be *badly* dressed, just that their clothes will be slightly duller, they'll be less impressive — in looks, appearance, the whole thing.''

Take Five: The shoot. It's 7 a.m., and a small army has descended on a downtown Toronto restaurant — performers, extras, cameramen, electricians, production assistants, a make-up woman, the agency executives, Merit's Ludmer, at least 30 people in all.

They're all there to create a 30-second commercial, and by 9 p.m. that evening, the job will still not be complete.

Aisha Films has promised the restaurant management that this sequence will be over by 11:30 a.m. — so the restaurant can catch the luncheon trade. Ossie, however, refuses to be rushed: Hurry can mean shoddiness.

"We face two problems," he explains, "the obvious one — telling a story and making a pitch in just 30 seconds. Then there's the fact that this ad is going to be viewed repeatedly, time and again, by thousands of people. They'll be scrutinizing it to the nth degree, and if we blow a detail, somebody's sure to pick it up."

Repeatedly, Ossie puts the performers through their paces, getting the timing of a glance, a raised eyebrow down pat.

In the afternoon, the action switches to the Toronto office of JWT. The ad team has requisitioned the agency itself as a location for the 'boardroom' sequences. Down the main corridor, normally a quiet oasis of corporate stability, there now runs a set of thrown-together tracks — along which the camera will roll as it pans in on a confidently striding Merit executive.

There's a brief cafuffle in the hallway as the office building maintenance supervisor appears to launch a protest. The looming set lights have been hooked to the building's power supply, and have already blown fuses twice. "Normally we use our own generator," comments a grinning electrician, "but we weren't able to bring it up 15 floors for this one . . . "

Despite the flurries of pandemonium amid long periods of boredom, everything is going fairly well, according to Williams. There've been no disasters like the time the agency was filming a beer commercial in Newfoundland, and used the brewery's own pub-lounge as a setting.

"We were using these big arc lights, and one of them was pointed near the sprinkler system — and the heat set the system off. You have no idea how much water those sprinklers let loose! And one of the electricians was behind the bar with all the cables — and here was this water pouring down, and things beginning to spark. He vaulted that bar — it could have been an Olympic jump."

Even though the Merit shoot produces no disasters, by 9 p.m. there still hasn't been time to film the outdoors sequence of two Merit men leaving a squash club. That will be done tomorrow morning for sure. Ossie *has* to get it done, because that afternoon he'll start working on one of the ads for the federal government's constitutional campaign.

Take Six: The 'answerprint.' It's two weeks later, in the lush screening room of Montreal's Astral Bellevue-Pathe film house. The inner circle has gathered again to view the almost-finished product.

During the past 14 days, Rawi has edited down the dozens of takes into one set of 30-second visuals. The Toronto music house has then created a sound track for it — an eerie but interesting combination of music and a breathy voice repeating, "Merit."

One last-minute change, creative director Hore explains, has been to use a male voice for the tag line — "Merit, the look that gets the looks." A female voice had been planned but "we went through the visuals and felt it would sound too sexy, too hard sell and obvious." Everybody agrees, the male voice does sound better.

The group runs through the commercial — an 'answerprint' which is still incomplete — several times, as agency producer Liepa and the projectionist try to get the sound track and visuals in perfect synchronization, since the sound has not been "married" to the film yet.

That will take place in the next week, as will the addition of overlays — corporate symbols, or dealer names — when the film goes to a photographic laboratory for finishing . . . *if* the client approves.

The client does approve, Merit executives and agency folk echoing each other's praise: "It looks good . . . the closing shot is a grabber . . . yeah, that music works."

The group straggles out of the screening room. All that's left are some final details: A last meeting with the client tomorrow, sending the film off for final colour adjustment, arranging for the completed ad to be transferred to videotape — the form in which it is sent to television stations across the country.

The group has spent dozens of hours and thousands of dollars — all to create 30 seconds, the Merit moment. ∎

Ad Info:

1. What are three major components of print ads?
2. What are the four main types of scripts that can be found in radio advertising?
3. What is the major difference between TV commercials and all other forms of advertising?
4. Reread the article on p. 75
   a) What is a production house?
   b) When is sound "married" to film?
   c) List the six steps in producing a television commercial.

Ad Data:

1. Examine a magazine or newspaper. Find one example of each kind of headline discussed on p. 63. Are there any headlines that don't fit these categories? If so, how would you categorize them?
2. Look through your collection of ads. What examples of action words can you find? What other words would you classify as action words?
3. Why might an advertiser create advertising that is only illustration?
4. Compare automobile advertising to advertising for a product such as toothpaste or laundry detergent. Does the length of the copy differ?

5. Look at the copy in three different ads for products or services you use frequently. Do the advertisers follow the four guidelines discussed on p. 65?
6. While you listen to the radio, keep track of the number of commercials by type of script. Which is used most frequently?
7. As you watch television tonight, record the different products and services advertised, and the type of commercial used. Bring your results to class. Using the class results, determine whether or not advertisers of similar products and services create similar types of commercials.
8. It is said that the best television commercials do not need sound to tell you what the product or service is and the benefits gained by using that product or service. Determine if this statement is true or false. Watch one television show tonight. Turn off the sound during each commercial break. How long did it take you to identify the product or service being advertised? Did you figure out the benefits? Would you agree with the original statement? Why or why not?

CONTROVERSY AND GUIDELINES

Because advertising is so widespread and so visible, it has an important effect on our lives. Governments have passed many laws and guidelines that regulate, in some cases, what can be advertised and what can be said in ads. For example, all beer and wine commercials must first be cleared by the Canadian Radio-television and Telecommunications Commission (CRTC) and all print ads by your province's liquor board. Most advertising must conform to the Canadian Code of Advertising Standards. All advertising on the CBC and CTV must first be approved by the networks. Almost all advertising follows the rules. Unfortunately, there are some companies that do violate the laws, or choose not to follow the voluntary guidelines drawn up by the Canadian Advertising Foundation and media. In addition, a number of areas of advertising, although legal, are the source of much controversy. In this section, you will briefly examine a number of legal issues in advertising including:

- gender stereotyping
- the portrayal of senior citizens and visible minorities
- alcohol and tobacco advertising
- advertising to children
- misleading and confusing advertising
- advertising standards

Keep in mind that only a small number of ads and commercials raise controversy or touch on sensitive topics. However, consumers do have legitimate complaints about some advertising. As a multi-billion dollar business in Canada, advertising will continue to generate both praise and criticism. In this section, you won't find right or wrong answers — only opinions. It may help to give you some new insights into advertising. To keep up, all that's needed is a keen eye and an interested mind.

Gender Stereotyping

A **stereotype** is a fixed idea or notion about a group of people. For example, for many years, women in advertisements were stereotyped as housewives, primarily concerned with spotless laundry, clean bathrooms, and the proper food for their family. To a certain extent this is still true. But, as some women achieve posi-

THERE WAS A TIME WHEN YOU COULDN'T GET A BUSINESS LOAN DRESSED LIKE THIS.

Remember when a suit and tie used to be a prerequisite for independent business loan candidates? A lot of fresh ideas were lost in the process.

Which is why, when you come to CIBC today, you'll find a bank that's just as forward-thinking as you are. And the people to go with it.

So whether you're looking for a start-up loan, or expert advice on

everything from cash management to payroll services, we're ready to help. And we're ready to put years of independent business experience to work for you.

Because at CIBC, who brings in the big ideas isn't what matters. It's what we can do to help.

For a more in-depth outline of the CIBC advantage, just call

1-800-465-CIBC. Better yet, stop in at your nearest branch and pick up your free copy of "FINANCING AN INDEPENDENT BUSINESS", or "FRANCHISE FINANCING".

 BUSINESS CLASS

We work for your business.

tions of power, their portrayal in advertisements changes. Gender stereotyping is not limited to women. When men are portrayed as helpless dolts who can't take care of themselves or manage a simple household task, gender stereotyping is taking place. The Canadian Advertising Foundation, through its Sex-Role Stereotyping Advisory Committee offers counsel to advertisers, agencies, and the media.

Seniors and Minorities in Advertising

The number of older people in Canada is increasing. Despite this fact, you will notice that almost all of the models used in ads are young and beautiful. Wrinkles or grey hairs are rarely seen. Most magazines try to have models from various age groups, but few models over 30 appear. This is particularly true in advertising fashion and cosmetic products. One advertiser explained that fashions and beauty are things that people dream about. People want to see what they could be, not what they are. Simply stated, beautiful people probably sell beauty products better.

The lack of seniors in advertising is not an accurate reflection of today's Canada. Seniors are more active and some more affluent than ever before. This makes them an attractive target audience for some companies.

Golden moments.

Sunny, quiet times. Days spent reflecting the love of a lifetime. Remember every golden afternoon on Kodacolor VR 200 film. Film so sensitive it can see the love sparkling in tender eyes. Fast enough to catch a fleeting smile. And so versatile that even in shadows, the light of your life comes shining through.

Kodak film. Because time goes by.

Another concern is the small number of ads that include representatives from minority groups. A study conducted for the federal government found that only 10 percent of the over 600 Canadian television commercials studied contained non-white characters. As well, in almost all cases, these people were part of a larger crowd, played a minor role, or were powerless or unskilled. In addition, the majority of visible minorities in the crowd were children.

The Canadian Advertising Foundation (CAF) suggests that the lack of minorities may simply be a reflection of the advertisers' efforts to reach a broad market.

Currently, the federal and provincial governments still portray more visible minorities in advertising.

Alcohol and Tobacco Advertising

Alcohol is one of the most heavily advertised products. Alcohol advertising is also regulated and carefully monitored. Where such advertising is permitted, each ad for an alcoholic beverage must be approved by the provincial liquor board, and, if it is to be broadcast, by the Canadian Radio-television and Telecommunications Commission (CRTC). The CRTC's regulations include restrictions on what can be shown in alcohol advertising. For example, drinking on camera is not allowed. Also not allowed are "youth symbols" (frisbees, skateboards, and stuffed animals). In addition, alcohol cannot be shown with any activity that requires special skills or mental alertness, such as auto racing or sports. Advertisements may not link social acceptance, personal, athletic, or business success to drinking a particular brand. As well, ads are to be directed to people above the legal age.

Some beer and wine commercials suggest that alcohol consumption and "fun" are connected. Such advertising is called **lifestyle** advertising, and is legal. In a lifestyle ad, the message says little about the product itself (such as its ingredients). The ad connects the product to some activity or to a glamorous and active social life. Compare this lifestyle advertising to the advertising paid for by the distillers and brewers to encourage people to drink responsibly, or not to drink and drive.

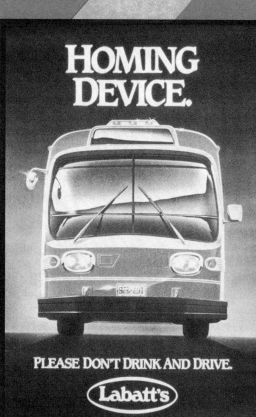

Radio and television advertising of cigarettes ended in 1972. The Federal Government has since legislated that there could be no further advertising of tobacco after 1990. A clause in the legislation permits continued exposure until 1993 of advertising that existed at the time of legislation.

Naturally, cigarette makers oppose a complete ban on cigarette advertising, and continued to lobby against the ban after legislation had been passed. The companies point out that banning advertising did not work in some European countries. In fact, smoking actually increased. The industry also rejects the argument that advertising influences people to start smoking. The companies went to the Supreme Court of Canada to argue that the ban on advertising violated their right to freedom of expression. Cigarette manufacturers claim they are only advertising to current users — encouraging them to change brands. The companies point out that the decision to smoke comes from peer pressure and family, not advertising.

Those against cigarette advertising note that cigarette consumption has decreased in England, Canada, and the United States since radio and television advertising ended. These opponents also state that although a young person smokes because peers or parents smoke, advertising does play a role in the decision. If advertising did not have a part in this decision, the critics argue, then lifestyle advertising with young-looking models would not be used.

In examining cigarette ads, you may have noticed that many include women. One reason is that these days more women than men start smoking. You may have also noticed that lifestyle advertising is used in cigarette advertising. Often part of the lifestyle shown in cigarette ads includes alcohol.

Advertising to Children

In ancient Babylonia, it was considered a crime to sell to children. Times have certainly changed! It is estimated that children see an average of 55 television commercials per day. The years between 1982 and 1987 saw the introduction of 75 children's television programs based on toy characters such as He-Man, G.I. Joe, the Smurfs, and Strawberry Shortcake, or wrestling stars such as Hulk Hogan. These programs are called 30-minute product commercials by some critics.

There is a Children's Code of Broadcast Advertising which sets out acceptable standards, but its principles are not always adhered to satisfactorily and further steps sometimes need to be taken. For example, as early as 1980, Quebec banned all advertising aimed at children under 14. This law was challenged in court by Irwin Toy. In 1989, the law was upheld by the Supreme Court of Canada. Why did Quebec take this action? Why was the province concerned about what children are seeing? Is children's advertising even a problem? Do children really believe what they see?

Supporters of children's advertising say that advertising helps children learn how to become consumers. They say that advertising generates discussions about which products are best to buy and why. Other groups are critical of advertising to children. They include a Canadian group, the Children's Broadcast Council, and an American group, Action for Children's Advertising, which notes that two-thirds of commercials shown during children's programs are for sugar-coated cereals, candy, cookies, sugared gum, and fast-food franchises. By comparison, only 5 percent of the commercials shown during children's programming promote bread, meat, juice, or milk products.

Most researchers agree that pre-school children are the most vulnerable to television advertising. Children under six usually cannot tell the difference between the program and the commercials. And don't forget that children under six do not use the other media for additional information about goods. Another study of young children found that:

- children attempt to influence their parents to buy food and toys that are advertised on television
- children, especially pre-schoolers, identify with attractive child models and want to have their food or toys
- children try to influence the purchases made by parents once every two minutes in a half-hour shopping trip.

Advertising directed toward children is unarguably lucrative. In the United States alone, sales of action toys increased from $52 million in 1982 to $872 million in 1987.

Misleading and Confusing Advertising

Although most advertisers are careful not to make untrue statements about their goods and services, some ads seem to make a big deal about something that is actually not very special, or make a claim that defies understanding. This legal practice is called **puffery**. Look at these examples found in an advertisement for an appliance store:

What exactly is a giant TV, and how can both a 20″ and a 26″ console be "giant"? Now to really confuse the issue, look again.

Here are a few other examples of puffery:

Gets your clothes whiter than white!

Is there really something that is whiter than white?

Now lasts up to 20% longer!

Up to 20 percent could mean one percent too! In addition, what does it last longer than? Other brands? Previous models of the same product? The Arctic winter? Sometimes advertisers use carefully thought-out words and phrases to avoid making claims that are untrue. Consider this claim:

This toothpaste helps prevent cavities.

No company can legally claim that its toothpaste prevents cavities. Nothing can absolutely prevent cavities. It is acceptable, however, for the company to claim that the toothpaste "helps" prevent cavities. The word "helps" is widely used in advertising.

Other words and phrases that are often used casually by advertisers include: bigger, better, improved, fights, stops, as good as, like. As consumers, we take these words for granted. When they appear in advertising, we rarely consider what they actually mean. For example, before you read ahead, think about what this claim means to you.

Our mouthwash fights bad breath.

The company cannot say that its mouthwash actually eliminates bad breath. By saying it "fights" bad breath, the message stays within the law. If you aren't listening closely, the claim can leave the impression that the mouthwash does eliminate bad breath. You aren't fooled by such claims, are you?

Advertisers also use photography to help make a favourable impression, particularly in the area of food advertising. Food has a tendency to go bad if kept under television lights for very long. Ice cream is particularly difficult to keep from melting! Therefore, special care goes into the preparation of food advertising. Sometimes the care food gets is better than that of a human model. One photographer spent nearly an entire day photographing chocolate chip cookies for a package!

There are many ways to make food look good. For example, ever wonder how cereal looks so good in advertising without getting soggy in the milk? That's because sometimes it's not milk—it's glue! Cereal doesn't go soggy in glue, nor does glue curdle. Other examples, all of which are legal, include:

- coffee keeps its fresh brewed look by being dabbed with soapsuds
- fruit looks shiny because it is coated in vegetable oil
- cooked foods are cooked only briefly, then painted
- hamburger buns are photographed with extra sesame seeds pasted on.

Not all additions to food are legal. One soup company can no longer put marbles in the bowl before taking pictures of its vegetable soup. The marbles pushed the vegetables to the top, making the soup look more appetizing.

Advertising Standards
The standard to which advertisers refer to ensure that their advertising is acceptable is the Cana-

dian Code of Advertising Standards. Briefly, the Code's contents are as follows:

- No ad may contain inaccurate or deceptive claims or statements with regard to price, availability, or performance of a product or service.
- Advertising should be clearly distinguished from a program or editorial.
- Bait and switch techniques are not allowed.
- No ad shall include deceptive price claims or discounts, unrealistic price comparisons, or exaggerated claims as to the worth or value of the product or service.
- Advertisements may not unfairly attack other products or services, or exaggerate differences.
- Advertisements must not distort the true meaning of statements made by professionals or scientific authorities.
- Ads for weight loss products or services shall include the message that such goods and services cannot work unless used with a balanced, calorie-controlled diet.
- No ad shall offer a guarantee or warranty unless conditions and limits are fully explained or it is indicated where such information is available.
- Ads must not encourage unsafe or dangerous practices.
- Children's advertising should not exploit children's lack of experience or trusting nature, nor should it present information which might result in their physical, mental, or moral harm.
- Products prohibited from sale to minors must not be advertised in such a way as to appeal to persons under the legal age.
- Ads should not violate community standards of taste, opinion, and public decency.
- No advertiser shall deliberately imitate the copy, slogans, or illustrations of another advertiser in such a way as to mislead the consumer.

When infractions of the Code occur, or when consumers find advertising offensive, the Canadian Advertising Foundation can be contacted.

Consumers have pressured advertisers to remove ads like these:

92

The advertiser isn't out to offend you. Advertising is intended to sell a product or service. If you are offended by the advertising, it's unlikely that you'll buy. And don't hesitate to let the advertiser know how you feel. Never underestimate your power as a consumer!

Ad Info:
1. What are five areas of controversy in advertising?
2. What is gender stereotyping?
3. What is lifestyle advertising?
4. What is puffery?
5. Name the code advertisers are expected to follow.

Ad Data:
1. Review the print ads you have collected. How are men and women presented? Do you object to the presentation? If so, how might the ads be modified to make them more acceptable?
2. Examine the ads you have been collecting. (You may wish to take extra time and do further research.) How many ads show senior citizens, members of visible minorities, or the handicapped? If shown, how are they portrayed? What conclusions can you draw from your research?
3. Watch Saturday morning cartoons. List all of the commercials during a 30-minute time period. Classify them according to the product advertised. What did you find?
4. a) Find five examples of puffery in ads.

b) During any 30-minute TV show, watch all of the commercials. Count the number of times the word "helps" is used in each commercial. Do certain types of products tend to resort to such wording more than others?
5. Collect current general interest and fashion magazines. Examine the way the models are posed. What do you notice about the poses? Review the information discussed about how women are portrayed in advertising. What conclusions can you make based on the ads you reviewed?
6. Examine any popular magazine (*Chatelaine, People, Elle,* for example).
   a) How many ads are there?
   b) For each, determine the probable target group. Is the product intended for use by men only? women only?
   c) Do any of the ads contain members of a group other than the target group? If so, can you explain why? How many of the ads include members of visible minorities?
   d) How frequently are men and women stereotyped in "traditional" roles?

e) What conclusions can you draw from this investigation?

7. Appoint a representative to call the office of the government department that regulates beer and other alcoholic beverage sales in your province. Determine the following:

    a) Can such advertising appear in all media? What are the restrictions?

    b) If advertising is allowed, what limits exist on the advertising? (For example, must food appear in the ads?)

8. Collect various retail advertisements from the newspapers. Retail advertisers often use the same words over and over again. These words include "sale," "over" (as in "over 50% off"), "off," "limited time only." What do you understand from the words? Do you think the advertiser wants to send out that meaning? What questions do you have about the meaning of the words you have identified? Re-write three of the ads in a way that expresses your interpretation of the ad. Compare your interpretation to two of your classmates'. Discuss why your individual interpretations were the same or different.

Ad Write:

With a partner, look through print ads and discuss broadcast commercials to determine if any violate the Canadian Code of Advertising Standards. If they do, you may wish to submit a complaint to the Canadian Advertising Foundation or regional Advertising Standards Council for your area.

1 2 3 4 5   4975-4   95 94 93 92 91